This book is dedicated to my dear wife P.

The Nurse Family of Bridgwater and Their Ships

by

James Nurse

Published by

Carmania Press

Unit 202, Station House, 49 Greenwich High Road, London SE10 8JL, Great Britain.

ISBN 0 9534291 2 1 First published 1999

British Library Cataloguing for Publication Data.

A Catalogue Record for this book is available from the British Library.

Artwork production by Alan Kittridge.

Printed by The Amadeus Press, Huddersfield, Yorkshire.

Contents

Acknowledgements

My grateful thanks go to Anthony Cooke of Carmania Press for publishing this book and for insisting that I should put pen to paper before it is too late. He also suggested a source for photographs showing the final days of the *Borderstar*.

Many thanks also to Eric Aldridge for the fine painting of the *C. & F. Nurse* which he has given me and which has been used on the cover of this book, also for the sketch of the *Borderstar*.

Also my thanks must go to all those friends too numerous to mention individually who have over the years assisted me with information, photographs and suggested sources of reference or contacts.

The late Harold Kimber started this quest for information on the family sailing vessels when he gave me photographs of the *J. Milton* and *Sunshine* from his collection.

James Nurse
Bromley 1999.

The Nurse Family and Their Ships

Background

It may come as a surprise to many people to learn that long after the arrival of the steamship and the railways, and even after the advent of the motor lorry, small sailing vessels were still carrying cargo round the coasts of Britain and across the seas to Ireland and the Continent. Of course, their numbers had been declining for many years but it was not really until the 1950s that sail finally gave up the ghost in the face of competition from mechanical forms of transport.

Before then, small ports all round Britain played host to whole fleets of small sailing vessels. They were usually owned by individuals or families, or by groups of relatives and friends, with each person having so many 'shares' of one sixty-fourth of the ship. Often the master would be one of the main shareholders. It was a tough trade and, at the mercy of the elements, many ships and men were lost.

One of the many families deeply involved in this trade – as seamen, captains, shareholders, owners – were the Nurses. They came originally from the Saul area of Gloucestershire. Many of them were involved in one way or another with the trows and barges which plied the River Severn and other local waterways. But, probably in the mid-1860s my great-grandfather, David Nurse, moved to Somerset. In all, I have been able to trace no fewer than 109 sailing vessels and 10 steam vessels where a Nurse was either the master, a member of the crew, the owner or held shares or a mortgage. However this book is about David Nurse and his descendants and the 20 vessels with which they were involved.

A rural scene at Percuil near St Mawes, in Cornwall, with the *Emma* being unloaded. Note the crew's laundry waving in the breeze and the horses standing in the water. *Author's collection.*

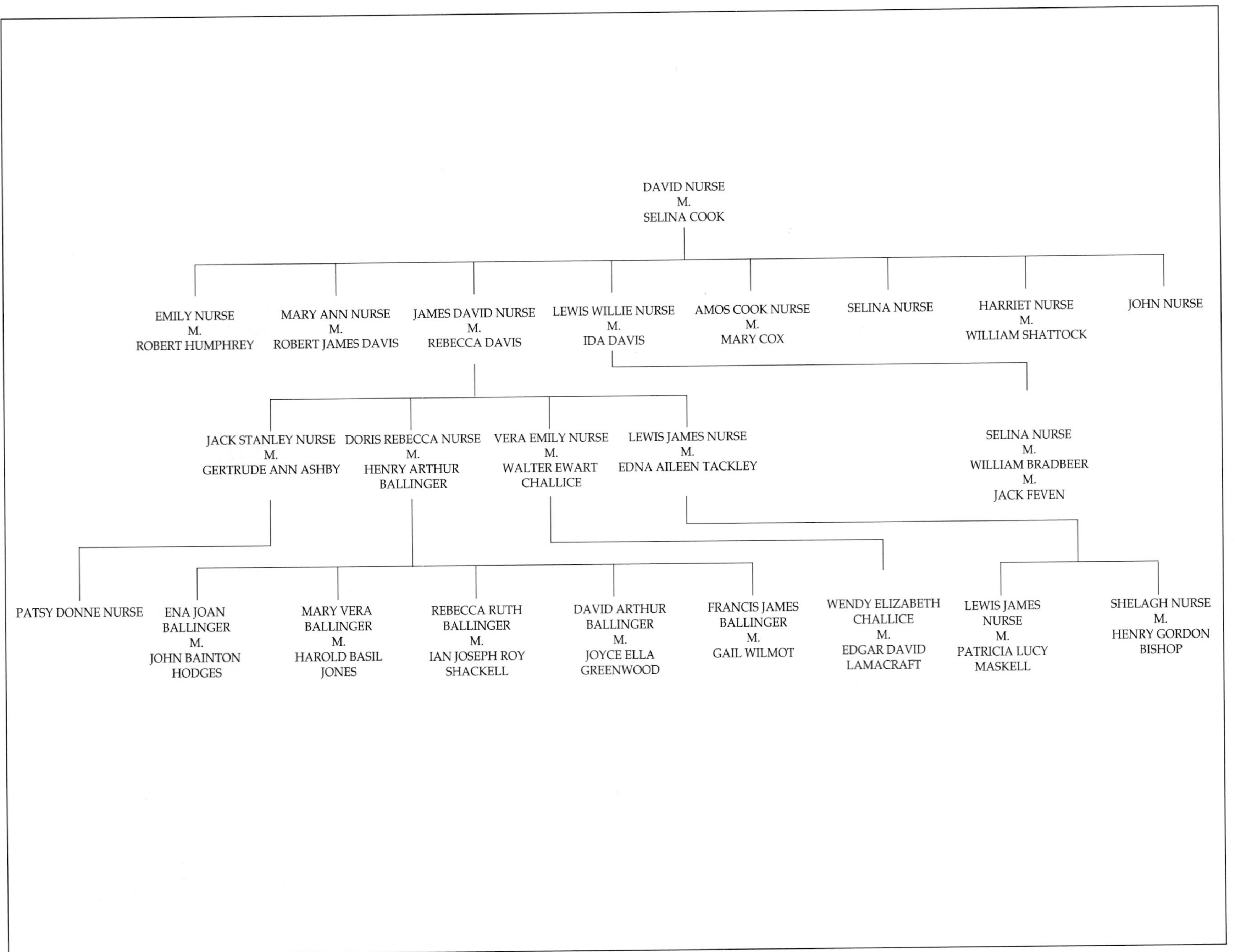

DAVID NURSE
M.
SELINA COOK
EMILY NURSE
M.
ROBERT HUMPHREY
MARY ANN NURSE
M.
ROBERT JAMES DAVIS
JAMES DAVID NURSE
M.
REBECCA DAVIS
LEWIS WILLIE NURSE
M.
IDA DAVIS
AMOS COOK NURSE
M.
MARY COX
SELINA NURSE
HARRIET NURSE
M.
WILLIAM SHATTOCK
JOHN NURSE
JACK STANLEY NURSE
M.
GERTRUDE ANN ASHBY
DORIS REBECCA NURSE
M.
HENRY ARTHUR
BALLINGER
VERA EMILY NURSE
M.
WALTER EWART
CHALLICE
LEWIS JAMES NURSE
M.
EDNA AILEEN TACKLEY
SELINA NURSE
M.
WILLIAM BRADBEER
M.
JACK FEVEN
PATSY DONNE NURSE
ENA JOAN
BALLINGER
M.
JOHN BAINTON
HODGES
MARY VERA
BALLINGER
M.
HAROLD BASIL
JONES
REBECCA RUTH
BALLINGER
M.
IAN JOSEPH ROY
SHACKELL
DAVID ARTHUR
BALLINGER
M.
JOYCE ELLA
GREENWOOD
FRANCIS JAMES
BALLINGER
M.
GAIL WILMOT
WENDY ELIZABETH
CHALLICE
M.
EDGAR DAVID
LAMACRAFT
LEWIS JAMES
NURSE
M.
PATRICIA LUCY
MASKELL
SHELAGH NURSE
M.
HENRY GORDON
BISHOP

The Family

Our family can be traced back to James Nurse who was born in 1760, but we start this story with David Nurse who was born at Saul in Gloucestershire in June 1832. In 1853 he married Selina Cook. The name Selina crops up several times in later generations, including my own daughter. The couple had eight children: Emily (b.1856), Mary Ann (b.1858), James David, my grandfather (b.1861), Lewis Willie (b.1865), Amos Cook (b.1867), Selina (b.1869) who died, sadly young, in 1883, Harriet (b.1871) and John (b.1873). John also died young, being drowned at sea in 1891 while serving on the ketch *R.T.B.*, then owned by his father and three elder brothers and at one stage commanded by Amos, although not at the time John lost his life. The Return of Death states that he accidentally fell overboard while standing on the forecastle head.

Like so many of his generation, David went to sea. In 1847, when he was 14, a crew agreement for the barge *Lucy* lists him as the ship's boy. He later served on the trows *Brothers* and *Sisters* and the galliot *Cornist*. The master of both the *Brothers* and the *Sisters* was William Davis and when, in 1854, David began his career as a shipowner – still only aged 22 – Davis was the other

David Nurse and his wife Selina with two of his daughters and a friend. *Author's collection.*

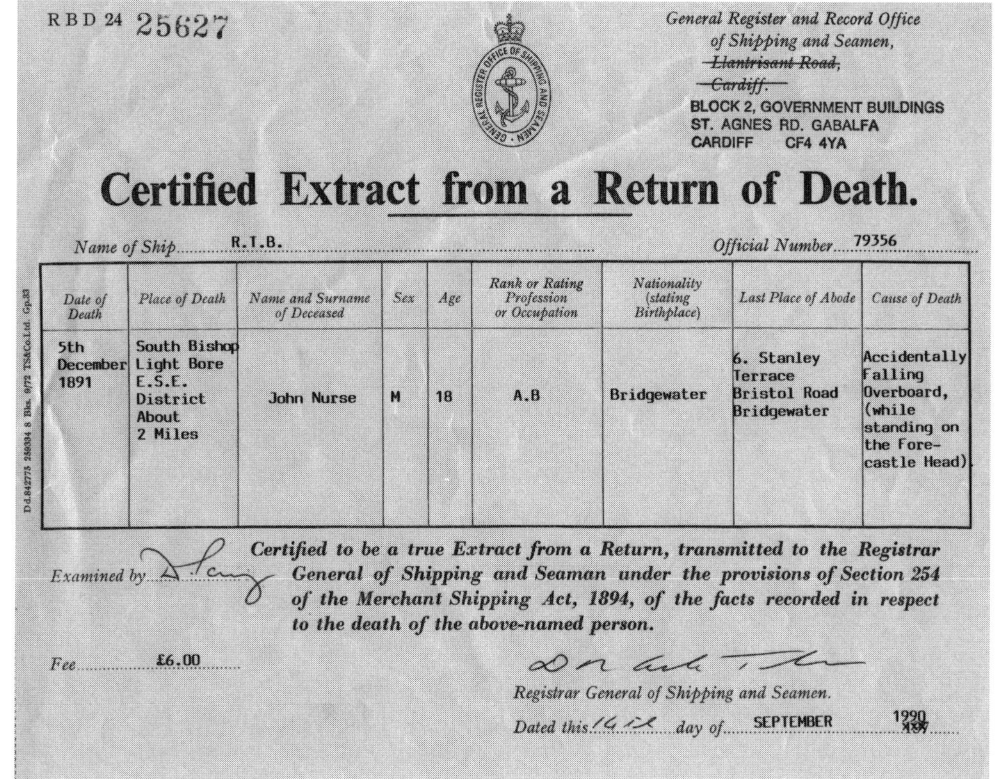

RBD 24 25627

General Register and Record Office of Shipping and Seamen, ~~*Llantrisant Road, Cardiff.*~~
BLOCK 2, GOVERNMENT BUILDINGS
ST. AGNES RD. GABALFA
CARDIFF CF4 4YA

GENERAL REGISTER OFFICE OF SHIPPING AND SEAMEN

Certified Extract from a Return of Death.

Name of Ship R.T.B. *Official Number* 79356

Date of Death	*Place of Death*	*Name and Surname of Deceased*	*Sex*	*Age*	*Rank or Rating Profession or Occupation*	*Nationality (stating Birthplace)*	*Last Place of Abode*	*Cause of Death*
5th December 1891	South Bishop Light Bore E.S.E. District About 2 Miles	John Nurse	M	18	A.B	Bridgewater	6. Stanley Terrace Bristol Road Bridgewater	Accidentally Falling Overboard, (while standing on the Fore-castle Head)

Dd.842773 259334 8 Bks. 9/72 TS&Co.Ltd. Gp.33

Examined by [signature]

Certified to be a true Extract from a Return, transmitted to the Registrar General of Shipping and Seaman under the provisions of Section 254 of the Merchant Shipping Act, 1894, of the facts recorded in respect to the death of the above-named person.

Fee £6.00

[signature]
Registrar General of Shipping and Seamen.

Dated this 14th *day of* SEPTEMBER 1990

A record of the death of John Nurse, lost at sea in 1891. *Author's collection.*

Amos Cook Nurse. *Author's collection.*

shareholder. The vessel was the *Industry* and the two men were equal partners. David was the master. At the time he was living in Gloucestershire at Framilode. In 1867, by now living at Bridgwater, he was part-owner of a sloop called *Grace* and I believe he was master of this vessel. Two years later he sold his shares in the *Grace* back to the original owner and, having also sold his shares in the *Industry,* bought a slightly larger vessel called the *Champion.* By 1876 he was well enough established to be able to afford to buy a second craft, the *Prince Albert,* which was commanded by his brother John. A third, the *Emma,* followed in 1878-9. She remained in Nurse ownership, with shares spread among the family, until 1917. Perhaps the most notable of David's ships was the *J. Milton* which he bought in 1889-90 and which remained in the family ownership until 1930. He also either owned or held shares in a number of other vessels, including the *Sunbeam* which in 1900 became the first of the David Nurse family ships to be lost – fortunately without casualties. But the crew of four had to remain on the stricken vessel, stranded on the Goodwin Sands, for nine hours during the night before being rescued by the Ramsgate Lifeboat. Owing to a snowstorm, their plight had not been seen and, of course, at that time there were no radios.

By that time, David himself had gone. He had died on the 19th May, 1897 and is buried in Bristol Road Cemetery, Bridgwater. His wife, Selina, survived him until 1916 by which time she was 83. She too was buried in the family plot. For many years the couple lived at Ivy Cottage, Bristol Road, Bridgwater.

All four of David and Selina's sons went to sea and we have already seen that John, the youngest, was drowned. The others followed in their father's footsteps, becoming masters and owners. Their eldest sister, Emily, married a mariner, Captain Robert Humphrey, but I have not found any record of his being master of any Nurse-owned ships. The other two sisters, Harriet and Mary Ann, emigrated to America. In those days it would not have been very likely that they ever saw Bridgwater or their family again.

The Three Brothers

Of the three surviving brothers, Amos figures least prominently in this story. In a generally long-lived family, he died at the age of 40 in 1907. I have found very little information about him. I had always been told that he had never married, but finding a gravestone in Bristol Road Cemetery with the inscription MARY, WIFE OF AMOS COOK NURSE, I started delving and found that in 1896 he was married at Bideford Registry Office to Mary Cox, the daughter of the local pilot at Appledore. Amos had been running into the ports on the Rivers Taw and Torridge at that time as master of the ketch *R.T.B.*. He is buried in Bristol Road Cemetery in the family plot. His wife had died in 1903 and is buried in an adjacent grave. As far as I am aware, there were no children of this marriage. There is a slight mystery about the whole thing. Why did the marriage, unusually for those days, take place in a Registry Office? And why was Mary never mentioned in the family? We shall probably never know.

The eldest of the three brothers, James David, my grandfather, was born on the 25th March 1861 at Saul which, incidentally, was quite an active centre of shipowning and operation. I have not yet found the first ship he sailed on, but a crew list of 1875 shows him on board the *Champion* as the boy, aged 14, with his father as master. In 1885, he was himself master of the *Champion.*

James David Nurse. *Author's collection.*

James David Nurse on board the *J. Milton* in June, 1923. *Author's collection.*

Perhaps James David's first venture into ownership came in December, 1886 when he and his brother, Lewis Willie, both took 16 shares in the *Sunbeam* which their father had bought the previous year.

In 1890, he bought the *R.T.B.* together with his father and two brothers, each partner having 16 shares. At various times he also held shares in the *Clareen*, the *Rose* (very briefly), the *Sunrise*, the *Esmeralda* (again very briefly – only for two and a half months), the *Speedwell* (a very old vessel, already rebuilt several times), the *Young Fox*, the *C. & F. Nurse* (perhaps the best known of the Nurse ships), the *Sunshine* and the *J. Milton*. In each case, he was in partnership with his brother Lewis Willie. The *Sunshine*, incidentally, was the only ship to be newly built for the Bridgwater Nurses. David Nurse seems, however, to have been in the habit of buying second-hand vessels and then having them enlarged or changing their rig. There were connections between the Bridgwater Nurses and their Gloucestershire cousins – particularly with Charles and Frank (the C. and F. of the *C. & F. Nurse*) and with Henry Alexander Nurse, described as a shipbroker.

In 1893, James David married Rebecca Davis by whom he had two sons and two daughters. The eldest son, Jack Stanley, born in 1895, followed in his father's footsteps until the First World War, when he enlisted in the Army. At the end of the War he returned to sea in charge of the *J. Milton*, but his war experiences seem to have affected him and in 1920 he collapsed on board his ship. He left the sea and took employment at Bristol with the Transport Department of United Alkali, which later became part of I.C.I. James David and Rebecca's second son, my father Lewis James, born in 1903, did not follow the family calling but took up farming. By then it must have been clear that there was little future for small family-owned sailing ships. Eventually he owned Benhole Farm, Stogursey, near Bridgwater, which after he had sold it in 1944 was to become the site of Hinkley Point Nuclear Power Station.

Rebecca died in 1927 but James David lived until the 5th March 1949, just short of his 88th birthday. Both are buried in the Bristol Road Cemetery. He had the reputation of being a hard case and a driver when at sea. As far as I am aware he never touched strong drink but he smoked a vile-smelling pipe. When my sister and I were young we took one of his pipes and tried to smoke it. We were both rather green afterwards and that is possibly why neither of us took up smoking. Even in his eighties, he was still fit and assisting my father on the farm. Every Wednesday, no matter what the weather, he would walk

Lewis Willie Nurse. *Author's collection.*

Jack Stanley Nurse. *Author's collection.*

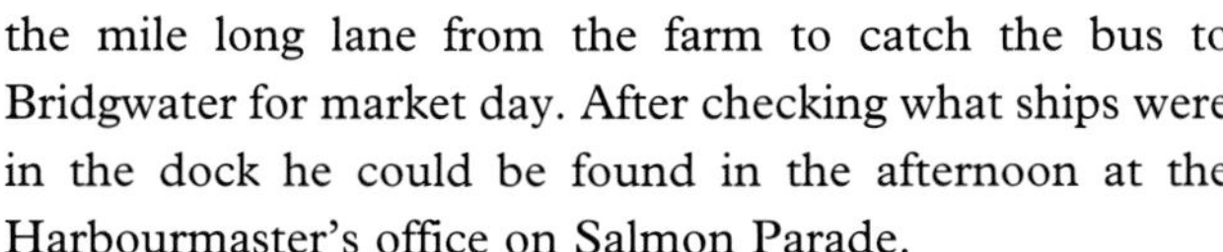

the mile long lane from the farm to catch the bus to Bridgwater for market day. After checking what ships were in the dock he could be found in the afternoon at the Harbourmaster's office on Salmon Parade.

Lewis Willie married Ida, the sister of James David's wife. Whereas his brother was a hard case, Lewis Willie was known as the gentleman of the family but it was said that when at sea he was just as much a driver as his elder brother. He could be very decisive. I have been told by my grandfather that when Lewis Willie was having the *Sunshine* built by W. H. Lean at Falmouth he heard that the builder was going bankrupt. He went to Falmouth, launched the vessel and had her taken to the yard of C. Burt for completion. I have been unable to confirm this tale though it has been told to me by other sources. The Lloyd's Survey Report for the *Sunshine* gives C. Burt as the builder.

By the time he was 20 Lewis Willie had become mate of the *Champion*, with his father as master. Later Lewis Willie became master of the *Sunshine* which, of course, he owned.

In addition to the ships in which he was interested with his brother, he was also involved with several other vessels. The *Fame* which had been driven ashore at Clevedon in 1915, was refloated by Lewis Willie and towed to Bridgwater, purely in order to strip her of her gear. It was almost certainly for similar reasons that he bought the French-built *Marie Eugenie* in 1927. On the other hand, he ran the schooner *John Gibson*, which he probably bought in 1904 after she had suffered bottom damage, until 1926.

In that year she was run down in the English Channel by the steamer *Empress*. Fortunately, no lives were lost.

Lewis Willie also bought the only steamship owned by the Bridgwater Nurses – the tug *Edward Batters*.

By the early 1920s, the sailing coasters were having to face competition not only from steam (and now also motor-driven) ships, but from the increasing number of lorries. Sail, however, probably retained a toe-hold in the Bristol Channel trades rather more easily than in some areas, since the lack of a Severn Bridge meant that road traffic between South Wales and the West Country had to take an extremely roundabout route, via Gloucester. Nevertheless, Bridgwater – like many small ports – was losing trade to a worrying extent. An acrimonious correspondence in 1921 in the columns of the local paper between Lewis Willie and James David on the one hand and S. J. Plummer, the local official of the Dockers' Union, on the other, illustrates this vividly. It was a time when workers in many industries were disgruntled and the Bridgwater hobblers had been on strike (They were the men who helped ships to dock and moor). By now with the port in decline, they must have been having a pretty thin time. Then there was the dispute over whether owners should be allowed to use their own crews to unload their vessels instead of using dockers. But behind it all was the recognition that the outlook for the port was bleak. Mr Plummer called for a steam tug to be provided.

The Bridgwater Steam Towing Company, Ltd. controlled by the Sullys and Hurmans, two other local shipping families, had kept tugs in the port for many years but had been wound up in 1918. Sullys themselves still had a tug called the *Bulldog* at that time so it is not clear why Mr. Plummer was calling for one to be provided. At any rate, in July 1922 a new Bridgwater Steam Towing Company, Ltd. with Lewis Willie as Managing Director and James David as a shareholder, acquired a tug called the *Edward Batters*. There is no evidence, though, that there was much demand for her services and probably her most notable achievement was to assist in taking the ketch *Fanny Jane* of Bridgwater in tow after her collision with the *C. & F. Nurse* in the River Parrett on 23rd, December 1931.

Lewis Willie died in 1936. Ida, his wife, died twenty years later at the age of 89. They had one daughter.

By the late 1920s, with the two brothers now in their sixties, the Nurse involvement in shipping began to decline. They sold their shares in the *C. & F. Nurse* to her captain in 1926 and 1927. (Captain Kelley, incidentally, was a strong character who had been master of the ship since 1909. He took delight in driving the vessel to her limit in all weathers and he is said to have been fond of eating raw kippers and Finnan haddock). Also in 1926, as we have seen, the *John Gibson* was lost. In 1930, the *Sunshine* and the *J. Milton* were both sold. By then, the Great Depression was under way and I suppose trade simply became too difficult. That left only the *Edward Batters*, which seems to have spent her last years laid up in Bridgwater Dock. She was scrapped in 1934.

Cargoes

The Nurse ships and their like carried a wide variety of cargoes. Very often it would be coal, probably loaded in South Wales, or grain, granite chippings and setts for road repairs, salt, iron ore from the Forest of Dean, occasionally timber. From London there would be either artificial manure from Lawes Wharf, Barking, cement from the works at Greenhithe, or oil-cake which was the residue of linseed after the oil had been crushed from it. Oil-cake was used in the making of cattle-feed. From Bridgwater the cargo would be mostly house bricks, clay land pipes, roofing tiles, household goods (by which was meant earthenware pots, etc.) and lastly, Bath bricks. These were made from the local river mud and were the forerunners of Vim and Ajax, They were mostly sold in bricks which were then crushed into a powder and used for scouring saucepans, etc. The powder was also used with colza oil for polishing brasswork, especially at sea as the oil helped to protect the brass against the moist conditions. It was still being used for this purpose when I was at sea in the late 1940s.

A ship's earnings were divided into three equal parts. One third went to the owners who paid all expenses (such as repairs, new sails, rope, paint and insurance). Anything left would be shared between the shareholders. The other two thirds went to the master. He paid the wages, dock dues, food and any other expenses involved. Anything left after these expenses were covered would be his own. For a careful master it can be seen that it was possible for him to save money in order to go into ownership himself.

Voyage accounts for the *J. Milton* for early 1913, relatively prosperous times. By 1929 many voyages were showing a loss. *Author's collection.*

Loaded at Poole Jany 1st 1913.
192. Tons of Clay for Runcorn
at 6/4 per Ton £ s d
Freight 60.14.0
Expences 3 10 0
Freight Clear £57.4 0
One Third £ 19.1.1

Discharged at Runcorn Jany 23.

Loaded at Runcorn Jany 24th
178 Tons of Coal for Truro.
at 7/9 per Ton £ s d
Freight 69 0 0
Expences 5 10 6
Freight Clear 63 9 6
One Third £ 21.3 2

Discharged at Truro
February 25th 1913

1913.
Loaded at Falmouth.
March 13. 193. Tons of China
Stone for Queenboro at 5/6 per Ton
Freight £ 53.2.1
Expences 4 11 0
Freight Clear 3)48.11 1
One Third £ 16.3.8

Discharged at Queenboro
March 22nd 1913.
Loaded at Northfleet
March 27th 192 Tons of Whiting for
Liverpool Birkenhead at 8/6 per Ton
Freight 81.12.0
Expences 9 11 0
Freight clear 3)72.1 0
One Third £24 0 4

Discharged at Liverpool
April 22nd 1913.

Epilogue

Although James David and Lewis Willie had ceased shipowning by 1934, three of their ships remained afloat for many years. Captain Kelley continued to trade the *C. & F. Nurse* for several years but in1935, after a brief period in other ownership, she was dismantled. The hull remained, however, and now called *Enterprise*, was used for storage purposes at Sharpness. By the 1970s she was abandoned and had largely disintegrated.

The *J. Milton* also continued to trade after being sold and passing through several hands, finally belonged to Joseph Rank, Ltd., the flour millers. She was no longer purely a sailing ship, as she had an engine fitted at some time in the early 'thirties. This was removed in 1945, however and she was then used as a stationary barge and later as a fender barge at the company's flour mills at Barry Docks. She survived until sunk in 1958 by a ship in the port and, although raised, she was scrapped.

It was the *Sunshine* which led the most exciting life after the Nurses sold her. She went initially to other Bridgwater owners and then to an Appledore man. She changed hands again and by 1946 was registered in Gibraltar and was operating in the Mediterranean, although still British-owned. Whether at first her activities were legitimate is not clear but these were times when some men found it difficult to settle down to respectable civilian life after their war service and saw opportunities for excitement and profit by taking advantage of the post-War shortages in Italy and elsewhere. At any rate, in May 1950 the *Sunshine* was arrested by the Italian Customs and taken into Genoa harbour. She was found to be carrying a large quantity of contraband American tobacco. Shots had been fired during the arrest and the *Sunshine*'s hull had been holed. As a result she sank in the harbour. Her owner, by then a Squadron Leader Berrington, was arrested together with the Italian pilot and eventually they were sent to prison and fined heavily. The Squadron Leader appealed, claiming that the ship had been arrested outside Italian territorial waters. The case was dismissed on appeal. As for the *Sunshine* herself, she lay on the bottom in a little used part of Genoa harbour until December 1953 when she was raised. She was broken up in July 1954. So ended the career of the last of the former Nurse ships to remain active.

Chronology of the ships owned

Minor transactions and mortgages have been omitted.

Key:	O.N.	Official Number.
	G/T.	Gross Tonnage.
	R/T.	Registered Tonnage.

***Industry** (1854–1869).*

O.N. 11657. Wood Trow.

G/T. 73. R/T. 51. Dimensions 65.6 ft. x 13.4 ft. x 7.2 ft.

(The dimensions varied over the years.)

Built 1825 at Stourport by John and George Ames.

1825. Owner John Adams Ames, Stourport.

1836. Sold to John Lovibond, Long Sutton.

1839. Sold to James Wood Sully, Bridgwater.

1854. Sold to David Nurse and Wm. Davis, both of Framilode, Gloucestershire.

1869. (March) Wm.Davis sold 16 shares each to John Nutt and Thomas Phillips, Newport.

1869. (May) David Nurse sold 32 shares to John Nurse (his brother).

1871. (August) John Nutt and Thomas Phillips sold 32 shares to Paris Thomas Dick, Weston-super-Mare.

1872. (August) John Nurse sold 32 shares to Paris Thomas Dick, Weston-super-Mare.

1874. (January) Liquidator of Paris Thomas Dick sold 64 shares to Frederick Charles Hipwood, barge builder, of Gloucester, who sold the vessel the same day to Samuel Watkins, Arlingham. He died 8-8-1874, his shares passing to Mrs. Selina Watkins, Arlingham.

8-2-1881. Vessel stranded and became a total loss at Burnham-on-Sea, Somerset, when bound for Bridgwater with coal from Lydney. Dimensions and rig for the *Industry* varied over the years. The above would appear to be the correct.

***Grace** (1867–1869).*

O.N. 56362. Wood Sloop/Ketch.

G/T. 76. R/T. 66. Dimensions 73.7 ft. x 19.1 ft. x 6.9 ft.

Built 1867 at Bridgwater by John Gough.

1867. Owner Geo. B. Sully, Bridgwater.

1867. David Nurse bought 16 shares from Geo. B. Sully. It is believed that he was her master at this time.

1869. David Nurse sold his 16 shares back to Geo. B. Sully.

3.12.1903. Vessel stranded and became a total loss at Yugs Well, Carnarvon Bay, while on passage Bridgwater to Liverpool with Bath Bricks.

Champion *(1869–1895).*

O.N. 10814. Wood Ketch.

G/T. 78. R/T.56. Dimensions 82.7 ft. x 19.2 ft. x 7.9 ft.

Built 1853 at Bristol by R. C. Ring, for his own use.

1869. Sold to David Nurse, Bridgwater.

1895. Sold to John Carter Hunt, Bridgwater.

1925. Sold to James Herbert, Saul, Gloucestershire.

1932. Sold to Tom Pockett, Saul, Gloucestershire.

1932. Sold to Severn & Canal Carrying Co., Gloucester. Believed converted to a barge.

1936. Sold to John W. Baker, Gloucester. Believed used as a house boat.

1939. Broken up.

The ketch *Champion* under a coal hoist, believed in the Ely River, Cardiff. *Author's collection.*

Prince Albert *(1876–1890).*

O.N. 10862. Wood open hold Trow 2m. / boxed Trow 1m.

G/T. 79. R/T. 53. Dimensions: 66.5 ft. x 15.1 ft. x 5.2 ft.

Built 1847 at Stourport by Benjamin Davey, believed for his own use.

1851. Sold to R. C. Ring, Bristol.

1876. Sold to David Nurse, Bridgwater. His brother John was the master.

1881. Rebuilt. G/T. 84. R/T. 78.
Dimensions 75 ft. x 17.7 ft. x 8.6 ft.,
now 2 mast ketch rig.

1890. Sold to James Tombs, Bristol.

1895. Sold by the executors of James Tombs to John Cook, Clevedon.

5-11-1903. Vessel sank in King's Roads, Bristol Channel, after collision with the *S.S.Coath*, of Penzance when bound for Newport in ballast. Crew saved.

Emma *(1878–1917).*

O.N. 45730. Wood Sloop/Ketch.

G/T. 80.6. R/T. 57.4. Dimensions 67.7 ft. x 17.8 ft. x 6.8 ft.

Built 1865 at Pill, Somerset. Builder unknown.

1865. Owners Wm. Vincent and James Tombs, Bristol.

1868. Sold to Oliver Camm, Saul, Gloucestershire.

1878. Sold to David Nurse and Benjamin Pearce, Bridgwater.

1879. Benjamin Pearce sold his shares to David Nurse.

1879 to 1917. Shares owned within the Nurse family of Bridgwater.

1881. Vessel enlarged. G/T. 80. R/T. 73.
Dimensions 78.2 ft. x 18.1 ft. x 9.2 ft.
Ketch rig.

1917. Sold to Felix Silvey, Epney, Gloucestershire.

5-9-1917. Vessel sunk by a German submarine which placed a bomb on board, 8 miles N x W from Sept Îles, North French coast.

The *Emma* (right) at the West Quay, Bridgwater. *Author's collection.*

The *J. Milton*, anchored at Falmouth in July, 1927.
David E. Smith Collection, by permission of The Trustees of The National Museum and Galleries of Merseyside.

J. Milton *(1889–1930).*

O.N. 65317. Wood ketch.

G/T. 100.54. R/T. 90.42. Dimensions 82.3 ft. x 21.4 ft. x 7.5ft.

Built 1872 at Saul, Gloucestershire by Frederick Evans.

1872. Owners Wm. Vincent and James Tombs, of Bristol.

1889. David Nurse, Bridgwater bought Wm.Vincent's shares.

1890. David Nurse, Bridgwater bought James Tombs' shares.

1891. Vessel rebuilt, believed by Frederick Evans, Saul.
now G/T. 117.32. R/T. 93.75.
with dimensions 84.5 ft. x 22.4 ft. x 9.5 ft.
The Arrival and Departure Book for the Port of Gloucester
shows the *J. Milton* arriving on the A.M. tide on 15-3-1891, her cargo being 5 tons of timber and spars and departing on the A.M. tide on 22-9-1891 with 185 tons of salt for Cork.

1889–1930. Vessel owned by the Nurse family at Bridgwater.

1930. Sold to Herbert J. Smith, Newport, Mon., fitted with a six-cylinder oil engine built by Thornycroft & Co. in 1927. It is believed that at this time the fore-topmast and mizzen mast were removed and a small fishing boat type wheelhouse was fitted. The hatchway was also enlarged.

1931. Re-named *Borderstar*.

1936. Sold to Grain Coasters, Ltd. (Manager, Herbert J. Smith).

1945(March). Registry closed. Converted to a sailing vessel (barge).

1947. Sold to B. I. Transport Co., London. Bill of Sale,12-3-1947. To be used as a fender barge at Rank's Flour Mill, Barry Docks.

1958 (March). Broken up after being crushed and and sunk by a cargo ship at Barry Docks.

The *J. Milton* being towed into Treport, France. Note the temporarily repaired damage on the starboard side. *Author's collection.*

The hulk of the *Borderstar* being broken up at Barry Docks, March 1958. *G. Deighton.*

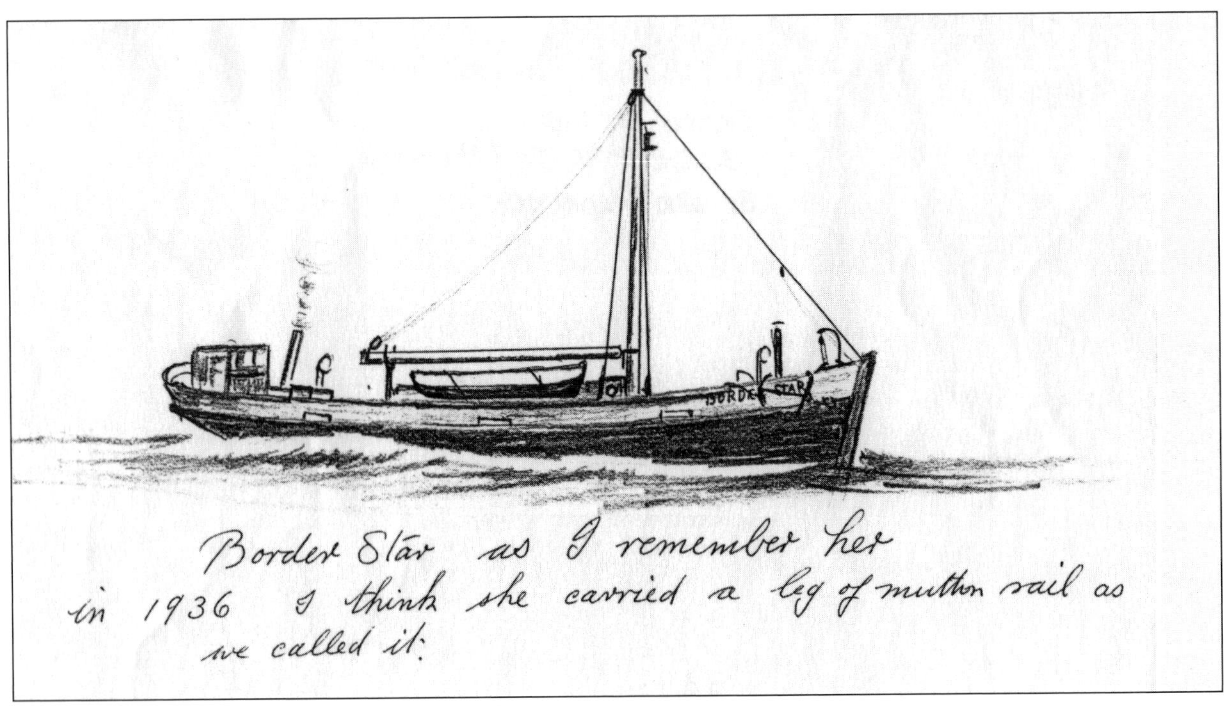

The motor coaster *Borderstar*, formerly the *J. Milton*. *Sketch by Eric Aldridge.*

Sunbeam *(1885–1900).*

O.N. 85809. Wood Ketch.

G/T. 96. R/T. 79. Dimensions 83.8 ft. x 21 ft. x 8.65 ft.

Built 1883 at Saul, Gloucestershire by Frederick Evans. Owner, Wm. Guy, Bristol.

1883. Sold to Rd. Williams, Stonehouse, Gloucestershire.

1885. Sold to David Nurse, Bridgwater.

1886. David Nurse sold 16 shares each to James David Nurse and Lewis Willie Nurse, Bridgwater.

10/2/1900. Stranded and became a total loss on the North Bank of the Goodwin Sands when bound for London in a snowstorm with pipe clay from Teignmouth. Crew of 4 saved after hanging in the rigging during the night. Her master at the time was Frederick Cook, cousin of the Nurse brothers of Bridgwater.

R.T.B. *(1890–1899).*

O.N. 79365. Wood ketch.

G/T. 82. R/T. 70. Dimensions 79.6 ft. x 21.2 ft. x 8.7 ft.

Built 1884 at Appledore by Richard Thomas Blackmore for his own use. Launched with sails already rigged and vessel stored. Sailed on maiden voyage two hours after launching. While under R. T. Blackmore's ownership she made a voyage to Gijon in Spain.

1890. Sold to David Nurse, Bridgwater. Shares split equally with his three sons. Amos Cook Nurse was master for a time.

1897. David Nurse died, his shares passing to James David Nurse.

1899. Sold to Alfred Hall, Bridgwater.

1900. Sold to E. Stephens, Par, Cornwall.

30-12-1900. Stranded at Aldeburgh, Suffolk, becoming a total loss, while on passage from Boston, Lincs. to London with coal. Crew saved.

The launch of the ketch *R. T. B.* at Appledore in 1884.
Michael Bouquet Collection.

Clareen *(1897 - 1917).*

O.N. 86521. Wood Ketch.

G/T. 95. R/T. 78. Dimension 81.9 ft. x 20.5 ft. x 9.4 ft.

Built 1884 at Plymouth by Richard Hill & Sons.

1884. Owned by C. F. Williams, Plymouth.

1897. Sold to James David Nurse, Bridgwater, who traded the shares within the family.

1917. Sold to Edgar A.Camm, Saul, Gloucestershire.

22-9-1924. Vessel lost on Church Point, Waterford Harbour during a gale.

The *Clareen* at East Quay, Bridgwater. Carver's Dry Dock is on the left of the photograph.
The National Maritime Museum.

***Rose** (1898).*

O.N. 85804. Ketch.

G/T. 94.22. R/T.64. Dimensions 86.3 ft. x 20.6 ft. x 8.2 ft.

Built 1882 at Bristol, Builder unknown.

Owner, Thomas R. Egelstaff, Bristol.

1884. Thomas R. Egelstaff died. Shares passed to Elizabeth A. M. Egelstaff (widow) and Julia Egelstaff.

1885. Sold to Thomas Orlando Egelstaff, Bristol.

1885. Sold to Edwin J. Rowles and R. T. Rowles, Frampton-on-Severn.

1889. Sold to John Fry, Bristol.

1889–1898. Shares and mortgages passed between various people in the Bristol area.

9-3-1898. Sold to Lewis Willie Nurse and James David Nurse of Bridgwater.

22-12-1898. Sold to Alexander Johns, Gloucester.

1916. Sold to Daniel Gower, Cardiff.

1918. Sold to Lewis Bull, Cardiff.

1920. Sold to George Head, Bristol.

1921. Sold to W. H. Bowater, Birmingham.

? Sold to Wm. Cooper, Widnes, and renamed *Dumas*.

18-4-1922. Converted to a lighter. Registry cancelled.

Esmeralda (-1899).

O.N. 28949. 3 mast Wood topsail schooner (Fruit Schooner).

G/T. 145. R/T. 119. Dimensions 97.5 ft. x 21.8 ft. x 11.7 ft.

Built 1860 at Brixham by John Richardson.

1860. Owner Shears & Co., Brixham.

1865. Sold to Wm. Sprague, Brixham.

1875. Sold to John Bovey, Brixham.

1891 to 1899. The shares in this vessel appear to have been traded between various people including the Nurses of Bridgwater and Gloucester.

1899. Sold to Alex. Johns, Gloucester.

25-2-1907. Vessel struck floating wreckage 10 miles SxW of the Kish Light, St.George's Channel and became a total loss when bound for Plymouth with coal from Glasgow.

The schooner *Esmeralda* waiting her turn to load granite at Calstock, on the River Tamar, some time before the First World War. *Author's collection.*

Sunshine (1900-1928).

O.N. 111391. Wood Ketch. Female figurehead.

G/T. 98.53. R/T.76.13. Dimensions 88 ft. x 22.3 ft. x 8.8 ft.

Built 1900 at Falmouth by C. Burt & Son for Lewis Willie Nurse, Bridgwater.

1900-1928.	Shares held within the Nurse family of Bridgwater.
1928.	Sold to Colthurst Symons & Co., Bridgwater. A 1927-built 2-cylinder semi-diesel engine fitted.
1943.	Sold to James Cox Screech, Appledore.
1946.	Sold to Barbara and Richard Havelock Clarke, Coggeshall, Essex.
1946.(July)	Sailed Appledore for Malta.
1949.	Sold to Sqdn. Ldr. L. Berrington, RAF., Bursledon, Hants. A 1948-built 8-cylinder Gleniffer oil engine fitted.
25-5-1950.	Arrested by Italian Customs for smuggling tobacco. Vessel taken into Genoa.
1951.	Vessel lying sunk at Genoa.
23-12-1953.	Vessel raised.
2-7-1954.	Vessel being broken up at Genoa.

The *Sunshine* at Bridgwater Dock. The gift of this photograph by the late Harold Kimber started the author off on his researches into the family ships. *Author's collection.*

A close-up view of the figurehead of the *Sunshine*, 1938. *Author's collection.*

***Sunrise** (1900-1916).*

O.N. 105408. Wood Ketch.

G/T. 99.65. R/T.79.08. Dimensions 83.6 ft. x 21.5 ft. x 8.5 ft.

Built 1899 by F. J. Carver, Bridgwater.

1899.	Owner Chas. Hy. Nurse, Gloucester.
1900.	Sold to O. C. Rudge who was her master (38 shares), James David Nurse (13 shares) and Lewis Willie Nurse (13 shares), all of Bridgwater.
1916.	Sold to Geo. G. Watson and Edwin W. Gill, Rochester, Kent.
1-3-1918.	Parted cable in a gale and drove on to a submerged wreck, lost her rudder, went onto a sandbank and sank while on a voyage from Charleston to Gravesend.

The *Sunrise* at Bridgwater Dock in October, 1912. *Author's collection.*

Speedwell *(1900–1913).*

O.N. 11724. Wood Barge/Trow/Ketch.

G/T. 68. R/T.57. Dimensions 63 ft. x 12.6 ft. x 3.5 ft.

Built 1840 at Droitwich, Worcs. by Joseph Jefferies for Harris & Son, Droitwich.

1855. Sold to George Mables, Worcester.

1868. Sold to Henry Guy, Snr., Newport.

1868. Vessel rebuilt R/T. 55.
Dimensions 73.8 ft. x 16.4ft. x 7.5 ft.
Trow rig.

1876. Vessel rebuilt G/T. 68. R/T. 61.
Dimensions 75.6 ft. x17.2 ft. x7.5 ft.
Ketch rig.

1892. Shares passed to Henry Guy, Jnr., Bridgwater on death of Henry Guy, Snr.

1899. Under mortgage to Charles H. Nurse, Shipbroker, Gloucester.

1900. Sold, shares held equally between Lewis Willie Nurse, James David Nurse, both of Bridgwater, Henry A. Nurse, Gloucester and Mrs. Sophia Cook of Framilode.

1913. All sold to Thomas Gilbert, Gloucester.

29-11-1917. Gloucester Registry closed. Vessel sold to be broken up.

John Gibson *(1904–1926).*

O.N. 73756. Wood 2 mast topsail schooner.

G/T. 106. R/T. 87. Dimensions 87.4 ft. x 20.6 ft. x 9.8 ft.

Built 1878 at Fleetwood by Gibson.

1878. Owner Porter Ship Co. Ltd., Fleetwood.

1904. Sold to Lewis Willie Nurse, Bridgwater.

11-1-1926. Run into and sunk by the cross-Channel steamer *Empress* in thick fog. Crew saved by the *Empress*.

C. & F. Nurse *(1911–1927).*

O.N. 109222. Steel 2 mast topsail schooner.

G/T. 119. R/T. 98. Dimensions 89.7 ft. x 21.9 ft. x 9.9 ft.

Built at Falmouth by W. H. Lean for the Nurse Brothers, Charles and Frank, of Gloucester. Keel laid down 1895. Vessel completed 1900. Yard No. 27. During their ownership the vessel made two voyages under Foreign Articles to Bilbao and Nantes in the Bay of Biscay.

1911. 32 shares sold by Charles H. Nurse to Lewis Willie Nurse, of Bridgwater, who became the Managing Owner. The remaining shares held by various people including James David Nurse also of Bridgwater, who later became the Managing Owner.

1927. Sold to Captain Kelley, of Nether Stowey, Somerset who had been her master from 1909.

1932. Sold to Ludwig Kristian Anderson, of Port Madoc.

1935. Registry closed. Vessel dismantled by John Cashmore, Shipbreakers, Newport, Mon. Hull sold to the Sharpness Dock, Gloucester and Birmingham Navigation Co., who used her as a barge and renamed her *Enterprise.*

1954–55. Hull beached on the bank of the Severn, up-river of Sharpness and cut down for scrap.

1971. Remains being covered by hard core to strengthen the river bank.

The *C. & F. Nurse* under full sail. This schooner had been built for the Nurse brothers of Gloucester in 1900.
Author's collection.

***Fame** (1915).*

O.N. 56361. Wood Ketch.

G/T. 65.89. R/T. 61.63. Dimensions 72.4 ft. x 18 ft. x 8 ft.

Built 1867 at Bridgwater by John Gough.

1867. Owner Charles Hunt, Bridgwater.

1889–1915. Shares traded by various people, with John C. Hunt, Bridgwater as Managing Owner.

13-1-1915. Ashore in a gale on Sand Point, Bristol Channel. Became a total loss. Crew of 3 saved by Weston-super-Mare lifeboat. Wreck bought and salvaged by Lewis Willie Nurse, Bridgwater. Gear removed. Hull sold to Bridgwater Harbour Authority, cut down and put ashore to strengthen the river bank at Dunball.

***Young Fox** (1916-1917).*

O.N. 98396. Wood Ketch.

G/T. 97. R/T. 80. Dimensions 83 ft. x 21.6 ft. x 9.1 ft.

Built 1893 at Goole by Cottingham Bros.

1893. Owner Wm. Boulton, Goole.

1898. Sold to Wm. Fox, Goole. While under his ownership the vessel made at least four long foreign voyages, usually carrying salt to Newfoundland and returning with dried cod to Spain or Italy. The crew on each voyage consisted of a hired certificated master, William Fox himself who was listed as the purser, a bosun, one A.B. and an ordinary seaman/cook. Mrs. Mary Ann Fox accompanied her husband on three of the voyages, signing on as a stewardess.

1910. Sold to C. J. and C. Symons, Bridgwater.

26-7-1916. James David and Lewis Willie Nurse, Bridgwater, each bought 5 shares.

1917. All sold their shares to Wm. Albert Jenkins, Swansea.

1920. Engine fitted, 50 BHP.

1923. Sold to Richard Mitchell, Polruan, Cornwall.

1926. Sold to James F. Voysey, Topsham, Devon.

1928. Sold to Donald McLeman, Avoch, Ross-shire.

7-12-1928. Ship missing, supposed to have foundered while on passage Sunderland to Portmahomack (Ross-shire).

The *Young Fox* in the River Parrett at Bridgwater. *Author's collection.*

The only steamship owned by the Bridgwater Nurses, the tug *Edward Batters*. *Author's collection.*

Edward Batters *(1922–1934).*

O.N. 124623. Steam Tug, screw.

G/T. 34.1. R/T. 1.04. Dimensions 54 ft. x 12.6 ft. x 6.6 ft.

Built 1908 by James T. Eltringham & Co., South Shields. Engines by Baird Bros., North Shields. Cylinders $10^{1}/_{2}$ inch and 22 inch, with a stroke 15 inch, 23 NHP., 140 IHP. 9 Knots.

1908. Owner: The Point of Ayr Collieries, Ltd., London.

1922. (June) Sold to Lewis Willie Nurse, Bridgwater.

1922. (July) Sold to The Bridgwater Steam Towing, Co. Ltd. (Managing owner, Lewis Willie Nurse, Bridgwater).

1934. Broken up at Newport.

Marie Eugenie *(1927).*

O.N. 81531. Wood ketch.

G/T. 51.79. R/T. 46.70. Dimensions 64.4 ft. x 19.2 ft. x 6.9 ft.

Built at Regneville, France, date and builder unknown.

1885. Owner F. J. Carver, Bridgwater. (Shipbuilder).

1885. Sold to Clifford Symons, Bridgwater.

1927. Sold to Lewis Willie Nurse, Bridgwater, for her gear. Hull broken up.

Appendix

Vessels on which David Nurse sailed before becoming part-owner of the *Industry*.

***Lucy** (1847).*

O.N.22996. Wood trow.

G/T. 40. R/T. 25. Dimensions 62.8 ft. x 11 ft. x 3.4 ft.

Built 1836 at Brimscombe by James Smith.

September 1869, Broken up.

***Brothers** (1848 -1850 -1851).*

O.N. 10808. Wood open trow/boxed 1875.

G/T. 41. Dimensions 64.4 ft. x 13.5 ft. x 5.5 ft.

Built 1847 at Brimscombe by James Smith.

Fate not known, but Crew Lists are in existence for as late as 1932 by which time the *Brothers* was 85 years old.

***Sisters** (1849).*

O.N.10819. Wood sloop.

G/T. 26. R/T. 20. Dimensions 38.29 ft. x 13.4 ft. x 5.3 ft.

Built 1815 at Broad Oak by Thomas Powell.

25-8-1881. Foundered in 10 minutes off Woodspring Point on voyage Lydney to Weston-super-Mare with coal. Crew of two saved in ship's boat.

***Cornist** (1852).*

O.N. 11624. Wood ketch/galliot.

G/T. 46. R/T. 40. Dimensions 54.7 ft. x 13.7 ft. x 6.8 ft.

Built 1811 at Chester.

10-10- 1872. Foundered in Morte Bay, Bristol Channel.

Registered at Liverpool, Beaumaris, Gloucester and Barnstaple.

The long-lived *Brothers* in Bridgwater Dock in 1911, moored alongside the *Welsh Belle* which was owned by the Gloucester Nurses. Behind them both is an unknown steam coaster. *National Maritime Museum.*

Sources

Arrival and Departure Book for the Port of Gloucester at the Public Record Ofice, Kew.

Crew Agreements at:

- Bristol Record Office
- Cornwall Record Office
- Devon Record Office
- Gloucestershire Record Office
- National Maritime Museum
- Public Record Office
- Somerset Record Office

Graham Farr Card Index

Library, National Maritime Museum, Greenwich

Lloyd's List

Lloyd's Registers

Lloyd's Survey Reports

Log Book and Accounts and Cargo Books for the *J. Milton*, in my possession.

Mercantile Navy Lists And Maritime Directory

Oliver Hill Casualty Lists

Oliver Hill Notebooks

Port Transcripts: For Westcountry Ports

Sea Breezes: Old and New Series

Ships and Ship Models